Good Health Guides

Food and Health

For a free color catalog describing Gareth Stevens' list of high-quality books and multimedia programs, call 1-800-542-2595 (USA) or 1-800-461-9120 (Canada). Gareth Stevens Publishing's Fax: (414) 225-0377. See our catalog, too, on the World Wide Web: gsinc.com

Library of Congress Cataloging-in-Publication Data

Fisher, Enid.
  Food and health / by Enid Broderick Fisher.
    p. cm. — (Good health guides)
  Includes bibliographical references and index.
  Summary: Discusses the importance of a balanced diet and the role of foods in good nutrition, as well as examining the eating habits of some typical sixth-grade students.
  ISBN 0-8368-2178-5 (lib. bdg.)
  1. Children—Nutrition—Juvenile literature. 2. Nutrition—Juvenile literature.
3. Food—Juvenile literature. 4. Health—Juvenile literature. [1. Nutrition.
2. Diet. 3. Food.] I. Title. II. Series: Good health guides (Milwaukee, WI)
RJ206.F56   1998
613.2—dc21   98-23245

This North American edition first published in 1998 by
Gareth Stevens Publishing
1555 North RiverCenter Drive, Suite 201
Milwaukee, Wisconsin 53212 USA

This U.S. edition © 1998 by Gareth Stevens, Inc.
First published as *All About Food* in England with an original © 1998 by Quartz Editions, 112 Station Road, Edgware HA8 7AQ, U.K.
Additional end matter © 1998 by Gareth Stevens, Inc.

Consultant: Dr. Martin Wright, general practitioner
Photography: Kostas Grivas
Additional photography and artwork: Sue Baker/Deidre Bleeze
U.K. series editor: Tamara Green
Design: Marilyn Franks

U.S. series editor: Dorothy L. Gibbs
Editorial assistants: Mary Dykstra and Diane Laska

Printed in Mexico

1 2 3 4 5 6 7 8 9 02 01 00 99 98

Good Health GUIDES

Food and Health

Enid Fisher

Gareth Stevens Publishing
MILWAUKEE

Contents

Introduction

We all look forward to mealtimes — sitting down to something tasty and feeling "full" when we have finished. Yet, we don't eat simply to stop feeling hungry!

Our bodies — and our minds — need certain types of food in fairly regular amounts to stay healthy. If we don't eat enough of these foods when we are young, we might not grow properly. If we eat too much, we gain unnecessary weight and risk the possibility of serious illness later in life.

Some foods, such as french fries and candy, have very little nutritional value. Filling up on these foods, instead of healthier ones, is not good for us. Luckily, many wholesome foods are delicious, too! Pizza, for example, has a crust made from grain; cheese, a dairy product; and plenty of tomato sauce. When it's topped with crunchy, fresh vegetables, it can be one of the healthiest food combinations around! We should always try to eat a balanced diet. It's all right to have fast food once in a while. Just be sure that, as a rule, you eat foods that provide all the nutrients your body requires.

Eating well is more important than ever when you're growing up. Sometimes, however, kids who think they are overweight go on very strict diets and might even starve themselves. Some develop a serious eating disorder called *anorexia nervosa*, which makes them very sick and bony-looking. We need to feed our bodies properly and get regular exercise to stay healthy and look good.

This book is about food — what's in it and what you need to keep fit. You are, after all, what you eat!

Balance

The more balanced your diet is, the healthier you will be and the better you will look. That's a promise!

Janet loved gymnastics, especially the balance beam, but if she leaned too much to one side, she would lose her balance and fall off. In the same way, if a person eats one type of food much more than any others, he or she is not getting a balanced diet and might "fall" ill. To be healthy and look your best, you have to eat well, which means eating a wide variety of foods so your body will get all the right nutrients.

If you don't eat properly, your body will suffer. For example, some people refuse to eat fat of any kind because they want to be thin. Before long, however, they start to get tired easily.

Q. WHY SHOULD YOU EAT A WIDE VARIETY OF FOODS?

your diet

They need to eat some fat because fat gives us energy. If a person gives up potatoes, bread, and cereals, he or she might feel very fatigued and could become constipated. These foods contain carbohydrates, which not only provide energy but are also a prime source of the fiber we need to complete the digestion process.

We can't cut out both meat and certain vegetables, either! They contain the proteins, vitamins, and minerals that keep our systems in good working order and our minds alert.

HEALTH PROBLEMS

Serious shortages of any nutrients can cause problems. For example, years ago, many sailors on long sea voyages suffered from scurvy, a disease that causes bleeding gums, skin problems, and anemia. Without refrigeration, they didn't have the fresh fruits and vegetables they needed to get enough vitamin C. Even

today, in many countries where fresh meat and vegetables are not readily available or affordable, people, especially children, suffer from rickets because they don't get enough vitamin D.

FIT FOODS

Fortunately, most of us live where there is a wide enough variety of foods to have a well-balanced diet. Unfortunately, many of our favorite foods don't, by themselves, have all the ingredients for good nutrition. A plain hamburger in a bun, for example, is mainly fat, protein, and carbohydrates. Yet, by simply adding a salad or some vegetables to it, we effectively balance our intake of vital nutrients.

Read that label!

Lots of information on bottles, cans, and packages seems to be written in a mysterious language! You can easily learn what it means. Here are some hints on how to crack the code.

Gary enjoyed helping his mother and brother with the weekly grocery shopping. When they each took part of the list, it didn't take them long to fill the shopping cart. Sometimes, however, Gary's mother sent him back to get another brand. "It's healthier," she would say. Gary didn't understand why — all orange drinks were the same, weren't they? Bobby, who was older, knew that a list of ingredients on bottles, cans, and packages showed they could be very different.

FIND THE FRUIT!
Bobby had discovered that "orange-flavored drink" actually had no oranges in it at all! A chemical provided its fruity taste. As for "orange drink," the label said only 12 percent was real fruit from "whole oranges." What Bobby didn't know was that "whole oranges" meant the skin as well as the juice. His mother always bought "orange juice" with a label that said it was 100 percent real fruit juice!

E-NUMBERS EXPLAINED
Bobby had also discovered that some orange drinks had extra ingredients, called additives, with mysterious names, such as emulsifiers, preservatives, and stabilizers. On some bottles, the additives appeared on the labels as "E-numbers," which are international codes for particular additives. For example, E223 is a sugar preservative.

Some food labels have a very long list of ingredients. In most countries, by law, ingredients have to be listed in order of amount, with the greatest first. So there could actually be very little of some ingredients in a can or package of food if they appear near the end of the list.

Q. WHY SHOULD YOU AVOID BUYING BATTERED OR BLOATED CANS OF FOOD?

SELL-BY DATES

As a supermarket sleuth, Bobby had also spotted dates, called "sell-by" dates, stamped on some products. A sell-by date specifies the last day on which a store should sell that food. In the past, food could be left on the shelves until it was sold. By that time, it might have spoiled. Some canned foods have a sell-by date that is several years ahead, but, as long as the cans are not damaged, their contents are safe.

Many producers of fresh foods now include a "use-by" date, too. This date is often several days later than the sell-by date, to allow for the time it might take you to consume the food after you buy it.

Bobby really enjoyed being a supermarket sleuth looking for foods with the healthiest ingredients and the fewest additives. The next time you go grocery shopping with your family, why not be a supermarket sleuth yourself?

The inside story

You could be in for some surprises when you study the lists of ingredients on cans or packages of food. See if you can find some of the following:

• **Artificial sweeteners**, such as saccharin or aspartame, are chemicals. They give food a sweet taste without adding sugar.

• **Preservatives** are also chemicals. They stop food from going bad, or spoiling, too quickly.

• **Stabilizers**, such as gum acacia, which comes from the tree of that name, give processed foods their textures.

• **Colorings** can be chemical or natural. Some chemical colorings are now banned in certain countries because they can cause

allergic reactions, particularly in children.

• **Emulsifiers** create a smooth texture. They are often used in products where, for example, rough chopped meat is used.

• **Antioxidants** stop fats and oils from becoming rancid. They can be chemical or natural. Vitamin C, which is also known as ascorbic acid, is an antioxidant.

• **Flavor enhancers**, which are almost always chemicals, can make mild flavors stronger. One of the most popular is monosodium glutamate, or MSG, but many people are allergic to it.

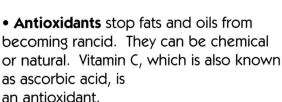

FOOD FADS

Do you sometimes refuse to eat certain foods that are good for you, then binge instead on harmful foods?

It was a hot day, and Edward was near the end of a run for charity. He couldn't wait to have a can of cola to cool him off! At the finish line, he gulped down the cola in a flash. Pretty soon, Edward felt as if he could run the whole distance again!

Edward's renewed energy came from the sugar in his cola and another ingredient that gives cola its flavor — caffeine. Caffeine is a stimulant that makes the heart beat faster. The energizing effects of sugar and caffeine, however, don't last very long, so Edward wanted more cola. Soon, he was drinking a can of cola every hour. Edward had a craving for cola.

If you don't want to eat certain foods because you didn't like how they tasted when you were younger, try them again. You might start to like them as you get older.

CRAZY CRAVINGS

Food cravings are caused by some of the ingredients, such as sugar, caffeine, and other chemicals and additives, in foods and drinks. Particular foods that many people crave, because they taste so good and seem to be very satisfying, start food fads. Unfortunately, many fad foods are often bad foods. Nevertheless, stores and restaurants try to make sure these foods are fast and easy to get or prepare when cravings strike.

WHO'S THE CHOCAHOLIC?

When you don't want a meal but can gobble up a whole box of chocolates instead, you're probably craving a chemical ingredient found in the chocolate.

Facts about fizzy drinks

A fizzy drink might look like a harmless mixture of lemon juice, sugar, water, and bubbles, but is it actually good for you?

• The "fizz" in fizzy drinks is called carbonation. It is produced by adding carbon dioxide to a liquid, then sealing the liquid in an airtight container.

• Alert! Many fizzy drinks have a high amount of sugar. The sugar is changed into acid by bacteria in your mouth, and the acid will attack your tooth enamel.

• When you're drinking something fizzy, the bubbles of carbon dioxide often join together and form a pocket of gas in your esophagus. The gas rises and comes out though your mouth — as a burp. Excuse me!

• As a fizzy drink passes through your digestive system into your intestines, bacteria that feed on the sugar content produce gas, which can make you feel bloated. Too much fizz can make you very uncomfortable!

Upset stomach

We all get stomachaches from time to time. Sometimes they are caused by a virus, but often they come from eating bad food. You can, however, avoid them.

"It must be something I ate!" Elizabeth wailed, as she curled up in agony, clutching her stomach. She had just vomited. "What did you eat, today?" her mother asked. Thinking for a moment, Elizabeth replied, "Well, for breakfast, I had those pancakes that have been in the refrigerator all week. Then I went shopping with Katy and grabbed a hamburger and fries at a fast-food place."

BLAME THE BACTERIA!

Poor Elizabeth! Either of these meals could have given her food poisoning. The pancakes might have started to spoil, releasing harmful bacteria. Her hamburger might not have been cooked thoroughly, or it might have been prepared hours earlier. Harmful organisms thrive in such cozy food environments and would waste no time going to work on her stomach. Then

Q. WHAT SHOULD YOU ALWAYS DO BEFORE A MEAL?

again, Elizabeth might have forgotten to wash her hands before eating.

EATING SAFELY

When you're eating out, you can never be sure how safely your food has been prepared. In this country, you are usually safe enough with well-known restaurants, because they have to follow very strict laws on cleanliness and food quality.

Some other parts of the world, however, might not have such strict regulations. So, although what they have to offer looks delicious, it might be safer to pass them by.

Whenever you do get diarrhea or start vomiting, remember that it's better out than in! Just be sure your body doesn't dehydrate, or lose too much liquid. Your doctor or a pharmacist can tell you what to do to prevent dehydration.

Constipation — the opposite of diarrhea — is another kind of stomach upset we all have at one time or another. If you have to strain very hard when you have a bowel movement, or if you can't go at all, you might need more fiber in your diet. Whole-grain breads and cereals and fruits, especially prunes, can help relieve constipation. Two or three dried prunes are a tasty snack!

BUTTERFLIES IN YOUR TUMMY

Sometimes, you might feel a strange queasiness in your stomach that is not caused by anything you ate. Perhaps you are worried or anxious about something and are having a nervous reaction that feels like butterflies in your stomach. You probably won't vomit or have diarrhea, and once the anxiety passes, the butterflies will disappear.

Beat those germs!

An attack of food poisoning can be agonizing. It could be the result of poor hygiene in the kitchen. Here's how to avoid it.

• Store all fresh foods in a refrigerator and don't eat them after the use-by date. Be sure to store cooked foods and raw foods, especially meat, separately.

• Always wash your hands before you prepare food and before you eat a meal or a snack. Germs flourish on dirty hands — and even on hands that look fairly clean.

• Keep food covered when it is left out, even if it's out for only a short time. Flies and other germ-carrying creatures, such as cockroaches, might decide to have a picnic on your plate!

• Always cook meat and fish thoroughly to kill off harmful bacteria that can cause food poisoning. Frozen chickens should always be thawed before cooking them.

special diets

How, and why, are some people restricted in the foods they can or will eat?

Geraldine's party was only a week away, but she still hadn't decided what to serve her guests. A lot of her friends didn't eat meat; one was allergic to wheat gluten, another was diabetic, and her orthodox Jewish friends might be offended if she served anything non-kosher.

Unfortunately, not everybody likes the same foods, and some are fussy about what they eat because they have to avoid foods that don't agree with them. Still others believe it's wrong to eat certain kinds of foods.

THE VEGETARIAN DIET

Vegetarians will not eat anything that comes from animals that have been killed. Sometimes, however, they will eat eggs and milk products, because these foods are taken from animals while they're still alive. Very strict vegetarians, called vegans, will not eat any animal products, not even honey. They eat only fruits, vegetables, and grains. Some people eat only fruits, nuts, and berries.

NO NUTS, PLEASE!

One food that seems to produce a bad reaction in many people is nuts. Children under five shouldn't have nuts because they might choke on them. Some children are allergic to nuts, and eating them can

Allergy alert

Do you like warm bread straight from the oven — and cookies and cake? Some people are allergic to these foods. Wheat and other grains, such as oats, rye, and barley, are dangerous for people who suffer from celiac disease. A protein in wheat, called gluten, irritates their intestines. A gluten-free diet, avoiding foods made with wheat, is essential for these people.

Culture also plays a part in what we eat. Most English people wouldn't dream of eating horse meat, but it is popular in France. A few African tribes eat snakes — and insects, such as locusts. Would you?

DIABETICS

A diabetic is someone whose pancreas, an internal organ near the stomach, cannot produce a chemical called insulin, which regulates the balance of sugars in the blood. Some diabetics can stay well simply by eating carefully. Others need regular doses of insulin to keep their diabetes under control. Diabetics also must eat at regular times throughout the day to maintain a healthy blood sugar level. Remember, too, that when diabetics say they need a snack, you should get one for them quickly. When their blood-sugar level is not right, they often get dizzy or feel queasy. A snack usually relieves these problems.

cause vomiting or skin rashes. Some adults have these reactions, too. A few people are so sensitive to nuts that the tiniest amount can make them very ill. They have to examine all food labels carefully to avoid nuts and products made with nuts or nut oils.

CUSTOMS AND CULTURE

Some people will not eat certain foods for religious reasons. Strict Hindus, for example, will not eat beef because cows are sacred animals in their religion.

Huge appetites

Japanese sumo wrestlers purposely gain weight for strength, but other people might gain too much weight because of a hormone problem. When people eat too much, their stomachs grow to hold all the food, and they find themselves eating more and more to satisfy their hunger. A doctor can recommend a sensible meal plan to help them lose some of the weight.

HARRIET

I don't have time for breakfast, so I grab a candy bar. For lunch, I usually have a peanut butter and jelly sandwich. In the evening, I eat hamburgers, and I snack in front of the TV.

OUR NUTRITIONIST SAYS . . .

Don't skip breakfast! Harriet should start her day with some fruit and cereal. The rest of her meals are too low on vegetables and too high on fats. For lunch, Harriet should try a salad or a turkey sandwich with lettuce and tomato, and maybe some yogurt. Snacking in front of the TV is fine, now and then, but meals are much more enjoyable when eaten with the family.

Who eats what?

Three sixth-grade students, all doing well in school, describe their meals on a typical day. According to our nutritionist, only one gets anything near good grades when it comes to eating breakfast! How foodwise are you?

Daniel

For breakfast, I can easily eat my way through a big plateful of bacon, sausages, eggs, and French toast, washed down with lots of ice-cold chocolate milk. I want to play football at lunchtime, so I usually wolf down a bag of potato chips with a can of cola. Sometimes I have a doughnut, too. After school, I always buy ice cream.

Q. WHICH IS THE MOST IMPORTANT MEAL OF THE DAY?

PAUL

I always have cereal, an egg, toast, and a glass of milk for breakfast. Lunch is usually something like chicken or tuna salad and fruit. Yet, by the time I get home, I'm famished! I'll probably eat three bags of potato chips before dinner. Then I have grilled fish, or a pork chop, with some vegetables, and I might have chocolate pudding for dessert.

OUR NUTRITIONIST SAYS . . .

Paul's breakfast gives him a healthy start to the day, but his lunch, although it is nutritious, needs foods, such as bread, to provide more bulk so he won't feel hungry again so soon. Then he might not have to binge on potato chips when he gets home.

OUR NUTRITIONIST SAYS . . .

Daniel must feel awfully sluggish after such a heavy breakfast, and his lunchtime meal is not at all nutritious. With little, if any, fresh fruit or vegetables, he is probably lacking vitamin C. All the fat he's getting from fried foods and ice cream isn't healthy for him, either. A better breakfast would be boiled eggs, toast, and fruit juice. A cheese sandwich, some carrot sticks, and a banana for lunch would give him lots of energy for football. Daniel should skip the ice cream on his way home and wait for dinner to eat again.

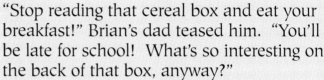

Valuable Vitamins

**When were vitamins discovered?
Why do we need each kind?
In which foods
can they be
found?**

"Stop reading that cereal box and eat your breakfast!" Brian's dad teased him. "You'll be late for school! What's so interesting on the back of that box, anyway?"

"It says this cereal is full of vitamins," Brian mumbled with his mouth full, "and there's a long list of them here. They sound good for me, but what exactly are vitamins?"

Brian's dad was glad that Brian sounded so interested in his food. "Vitamins," he explained, "are natural substances our bodies need to stay healthy. Our bodies either can't make them or don't produce the amounts we need, so we have to get them from food. Our bodies can't store all the vitamins we need, either, so we should eat foods that contain certain vitamins every day."

Brian's dad also told him that the most important vitamins are A, B complex (so-called because there are a lot of them), C, D, E, and K. He wasn't sure what to say, however, when Brian asked him when vitamins were discovered. Actually, scientists first coined the word "vitamin" in 1912.

ALTOGETHER NOW!
There are thirteen vitamins altogether. "Why do we need all of them?" Brian asked. "Isn't one enough?"

Q. WHY DO WE NEED SO MANY TYPES OF VITAMINS?

Know your vitamins

A balanced diet, and a little sunshine, should give you all of the following essential vitamins.

Vitamin A is good for your eyesight, skin, and immune system. You can find it in oily fish, such as sardines and tuna, as well as in eggs and butter.

Vitamin D is essential for strong, healthy bones. You will find it in milk, oily fish, and meat — and sunlight helps produce it.

Vitamin B complex is good for your lungs and nervous system. It is found in meat, nuts, and dairy foods.

Vitamin E, which is found in whole-grain bread, is especially good for your skin and will help keep you looking your best.

Vitamin C, found in fruits and vegetables, helps fight infection and is good for your skin. Your body cannot store it, so you need it every day.

Vitamin K helps your blood clot when you cut yourself. Eat plenty of greens, such as spinach and broccoli, to get it! Greens are a valuable source of this important vitamin.

"No," said his dad. "We need all the vitamins because each one does something different. Some keep our skin healthy; others boost our immune systems or give us strong bones; still others help our blood clot when we cut ourselves, or keep our nervous systems in good condition. We can get the vitamins we need only if we eat a wide variety of foods.

"Vegetables have a lot of valuable vitamins. Unfortunately, many of them are lost if the vegetables are overcooked. So we can get more vitamins from our vegetables if we eat them raw."

The chart on this page lists most of the major vitamins, the foods that contain them, and the benefits of each. Why not study it and get vitamin-wise — like Brian!

Minerals

Why do we need minerals? In which foods will we find them? If we don't eat all these foods, should we take a mineral supplement?

"The container says there's iron in this milk shake," Diane said suspiciously, "but I don't see any pieces of iron in it! I thought iron was used to make porch railings!"

Diane might be surprised to learn that many elements found in the ground turn up in the foods we eat. They are known as minerals, and our bodies need them to function properly. *Calcium*, for example, is a silvery-white metallic element that, in extremely small amounts, is vital for the development of healthy bones, teeth, muscles, and nerves. Calcium is found in some green vegetables, eggs, fish, and dairy products, such as milk, butter, and cheese.

Minerals on the menu

Write down everything you ate yesterday and check which minerals the main items on your menu contained.

You need **calcium** to build strong bones. A lack of calcium can make your bones brittle.

Q. CAN YOU TAKE TOO MUCH OF A MINERAL SUPPLEMENT?

matter

THE METAL IN YOUR MEALS

Zinc, in small amounts, keeps skin healthy and immune systems in good working order. We can get it by eating meats, seafood, and bananas.

Potassium, which is found in most fruits, vegetables, meat, and fish, is essential for good blood circulation. Table salt contains two vital minerals, *sodium* and *chloride*. We need both of these minerals in small quantities; too much can raise our blood pressure.

Although Diane couldn't see any "pieces" of iron in her milk shake, iron was an ingredient — in a different form. *Iron* is found in a wide variety of foods, such as meat, liver, spinach, and whole-grain bread. It keeps our blood healthy. We need *copper*, too, from meat, whole-grain cereals, soybeans, and seafood. *Phosphorus* is good for teeth and bones. It is found in eggs, fish, and dairy foods.

If we don't eat all of these foods, it is possible to miss out on some important minerals. A mineral supplement can help but should be taken only in the recommended dose or in an amount prescribed for you by a doctor.

Calcium, fluoride, and phosphorus are often added to toothpaste to help create a winning smile.

A healthy heart, good circulation, and blood rich in red cells require **iron** and **potassium**.

Carbohydrates COUNT

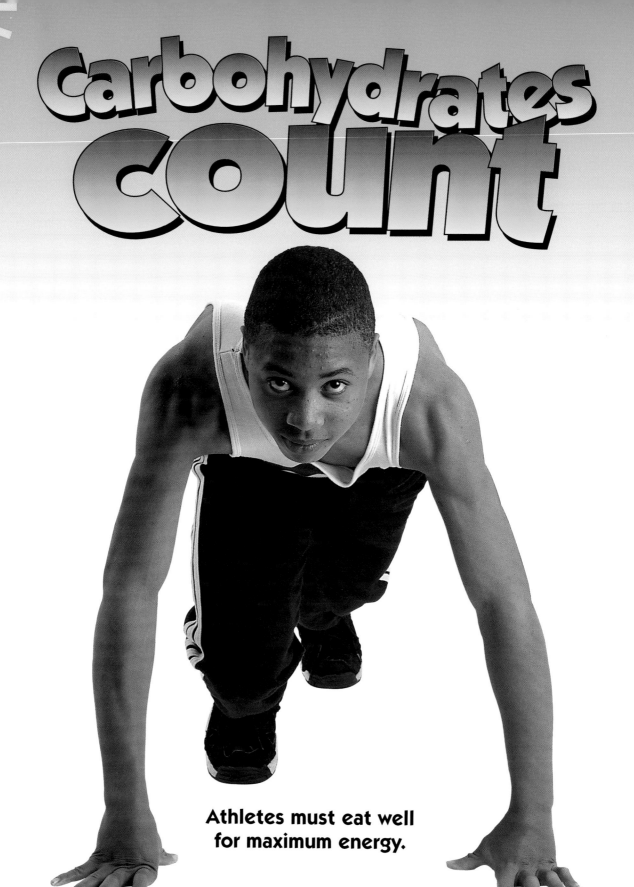

Athletes must eat well for maximum energy.

Q. WHY IS A BAKED POTATO HEALTHIER THAN FRENCH FRIES?

"French fries are fattening," Joe's mother reminded him, "so don't have too many for lunch!"

"Rats!" thought Joe. "I was looking forward to having some. They fill me up, and they're really cheap, too."

Joe knew his mother was right, though. He'd eaten french fries every day last week, and he was starting to feel fat. He wished french fries were a healthy food! Joe should know that potatoes are actually very healthy; it's the fat fries are cooked in that piles on the pounds.

ENERGY FOODS

Joe plays a lot of sports, so his body needs foods like potatoes, bread, rice, and pasta for energy. They are rich in carbohydrates. Carbohydrates are found in sugars, too, either refined sugar, the kind we keep in the sugar bowl, or natural sugars, such as those present in fresh fruit.

At one time, Joe would have been told that the way to keep his weight down was not to eat carbohydrate foods. We know now that not eating carbohydrates would make Joe feel tired. That's why Joe's mother gives him whole-grain bread and cereal for breakfast. She knows they contain enough carbohydrates to keep Joe running at top speed for hours!

ONLY A BOOST

Why won't sugary foods, which also are carbohydrates, make Joe feel just as lively? Unfortunately, the carbohydrate content of sugars might give us a quick boost, but it cannot maintain energy levels over longer periods of time.

People who don't exercise very much can have too many carbohydrates in their diets, but athletes and sportsmen are different. They need a lot of carbohydrate foods to replace the energy they use up. If they relied on fats to give them energy, they'd double their weight in no time! In the future, Joe would be wise to have a healthy baked potato, instead of french fries.

Facts about fats

A diet that cuts out all fats is not healthy. Your body needs a certain amount of fat to function properly, and some fats are actually good for you.

Q. HOW CAN VEGETARIANS GET THE HEALTHY FATS THEY NEED?

Good fats, bad fats

Some fats are healthier than others. Which are the healthiest? Which are the most harmful?

Sinister saturates

Meat, dairy products, and some vegetable oils, such as palm oil and coconut oil, are full of **saturated** fats and are high in calories. We need them in reasonable amounts, but too much can be harmful. Many candies, as well as chocolate, rich ice cream, cakes, and cookies also can have high levels of saturated fat.

Alternative oils

Some types of fat, such as olive oil; cooking oils made from crushed sunflower seeds, corn, or rapeseeds; and the fat found in oily fish, are good for us! They contain essential fatty acids, which help keep our nervous systems healthy.

Alternative oils contain **monounsaturated** or **polyunsaturated** fats, which do not leave as much fat deposited inside our blood vessels. We take in a lot of fat when we eat fried foods, but using sunflower or olive oil, both of which are high in monounsaturated fat, is healthier than using butter or lard.

Clobber that cholesterol!

One substance we hear a lot about these days — **cholesterol** — often takes the blame for heart trouble. Cholesterol is produced naturally by the body. We need it, but we might have too much of it if we eat too many high-cholesterol foods, such as eggs, butter, and shellfish. Some foods, such as olive oil, can actually reduce the amount of cholesterol in our blood!

Tess felt overweight, so she decided to start exercising regularly and to eat absolutely no fat. No fat meant no french fries, no buttered toast, no ice cream. None! Was she right? In some ways, yes. When we exercise, fat is used for energy; any left over is stored in our body cells. If we don't exercise enough, the fat we eat continues to be stored, and our bodies get bigger. Eating no fat at all, however, could make us sick! Our bodies can absorb some vitamins and minerals only through the fats in our diets. Tess needs to eat some fat to stay healthy; she just has to cut down on the amount and avoid certain types of fat, as described on this page.

Protein

A well-balanced meal will contain lots of vegetables, some carbohydrates, and a moderate amount of an incredible bodybuilding substance called protein.

Darren heard a crash outside his bedroom window. He looked out and saw that his neighbor's garden shed had collapsed. Darren was not surprised. He had watched his neighbor building it a few years earlier. It was a flimsy wooden structure that had not been kept in good repair and had started to rot.

The human body also needs to be kept in good repair. To do that, we must eat proteins. Proteins are substances that help us grow and keep our bodies strong.

THE BODY'S BUILDING BLOCKS
Proteins are often called "building blocks" because they consist of chains of organic compounds known as amino acids. Our bodies need the amino acids in proteins to keep systems, such as circulation and digestion, running smoothly. We also need them for growth and to repair body tissues.

Q. HOW CAN VEGETARIANS GET PROTEIN IF THEY ARE ALLERGIC TO NUTS?

power

Our bodies can make some amino acids, but those we can't make, we must get from the foods we eat.

PICK YOUR PROTEIN

Proteins can be found in a variety of foods. Meats, dairy products, eggs, fish, and cereals are full of protein. Nuts are high in proteins, too — ideal for vegetarians!

Not all foods, however, contain the same kinds of proteins. The proteins found in animal products — almost all types of meat, dairy foods, and eggs — are absorbed more readily by the body than those found in grains and vegetables such as peas, beans, and lentils. Yet meat is not an essential food. We can get protein equally as valuable from food sources that are not animal products.

HOW MUCH PROTEIN DO I NEED?

You don't have to pile your plate with big chunks of meat or fish to get the protein your body requires. In fact, it is better to have more vegetables than protein on your plate. Although you don't need a lot of protein, you should eat a reasonable amount at least once or twice a day.

An ideal meal

Eating grain and vegetable foods together, such as baked beans on toast, produces a combination of proteins just as nutritious as those found in beef, ham, chicken, or fish. So vegetarians need never lack protein power!

A. BAKED BEANS ARE A GOOD SOURCE OF PROTEIN FOR VEGETARIANS, TOO.

Food magic

There are some widely-held beliefs about the benefits
and drawbacks of certain foods. Are they true?
A nutritionist puts it all into perspective.

IS IT TRUE THAT GARLIC HAS HEALTH-GIVING PROPERTIES?

Garlic, which belongs to the same vegetable family as the onion, contains a substance called *allyl disulphide* that helps the blood break down clots that might otherwise lead to severe health problems. Garlic is also believed to help lower cholesterol levels in the blood. Some people claim that garlic can help prevent common colds, too. Garlic pills are available for these purposes, and they don't leave a strong garlic odor on the breath the way eating the vegetable itself does.

WILL AN APPLE A DAY REALLY KEEP THE DOCTOR AWAY?

An apple tastes fresh and healthy, but, nutritionally, it is of little value. Only a tenth of an apple is carbohydrates, and the protein and fiber content is very small, too. On the plus side, an apple has no fat, and it does contain vitamins B and C, which are good for the immune system and help fight infections. So we might not have to see the doctor as often if we eat apples regularly. Apples, however, do not provide all the vitamins we need, so we must eat many other foods, too. Eating an apple a day might, however, keep the *dentist* away. Its crunchy texture is good for teeth to bite into and helps teeth stay healthy.

Q. WHY IS AN APPLE A BETTER SNACK THAN CANDY?

IS IT TRUE THAT SOME FOODS CAN CAUSE ZITS?

No single food, unless you're allergic to it, will cause pimples or acne if you eat only small amounts of it. If, however, you continually eat fatty, fried foods or foods full of sugar, such as candy and soft drinks, some of the fats and sugars are deposited in your bloodstream, making your blood very rich — which might aggravate zits. So cut down on fried and sugary foods.

IS RAW FOOD HEALTHIER THAN COOKED FOOD?

Some foods are healthier eaten raw because the cooking process destroys many of their nutrients. All food should, at least, be washed before eating, and some fruits and vegetables need to be peeled because their skins are not edible.

Some foods, however, must be cooked to destroy germs or toxins. Raw chicken, for example, might have *salmonella* bacteria, but thorough cooking will kill it and make the meat safe to eat. Some beans must also be cooked to destroy toxins.

ARE PROCESSED FOODS BAD FOR US?

Many of today's processed foods are convenience foods. They contain additives to help preserve them, give them color and texture, and provide additional nutrients. Most additives are, by law, present only in very small amounts and are not harmful to most people. Some people, however, are allergic to particular chemicals and might become quite ill after eating certain processed foods. These people are better off sticking with fresh foods.

Processing does, however, have its pluses. In fact, most foods go through some kind of processing between the time they are harvested or killed and the time they reach the supermarket. This processing keeps them fresh. Fruit and vegetables, for example, might be canned or heat-treated to make them last longer, or they might be frozen. Frozen produce might even be fresher when you eat it, than produce "fresh" from the store, because it was processed immediately after picking. Some forms of processing destroy harmful bacteria that would otherwise make us ill if we ate them in our foods.

A. APPLES ARE BETTER FOR YOUR TEETH THAN CANDY.

Glossary

additive — a natural or artificial ingredient added to foods in small amounts to produce a desired change, such as a stronger flavor or more appetizing texture.

anemia — a health condition in which a person lacks energy and becomes tired easily because his or her blood is not producing enough oxygen-carrying red cells.

anorexia nervosa — a serious eating problem that causes a person to lose too much weight.

bloated — abnormally puffed up or swollen, usually with air or water.

caffeine — a chemical ingredient commonly found in coffee, tea, and cola drinks that speeds up the heart and nervous system.

carbohydrate — a chemical compound, in foods containing sugars, starches, and fiber, that gives the body energy.

cholesterol — a kind of animal fat, found in some foods and produced naturally by the body, that can clog blood vessels and cause poor circulation and heart attacks.

diabetes — a disease in which the body is unable to produce the insulin it needs to balance the amount of sugars present in the bloodstream.

diarrhea — unusually frequent and fluid bowel movements.

fiber — material in foods, such as fruits, vegetables, and grains, that is not digested, but helps carry the food through the intestines.

gluten — a tough, elastic protein substance found in wheat flour that helps the dough stick together.

insulin — a hormone produced by the pancreas that helps the body use sugars and starches, or carbohydrates, for energy and growth.

nutrient — a substance, such as a vitamin, mineral, or protein, that living things need to grow and stay healthy.

protein — a chemical compound, in foods such as meat, eggs, cheese, nuts, and beans, that is needed to help grow and repair body tissue.

rancid — having a bad or sour smell due to spoiling or rotting.

rickets — a children's disease in which their bones become soft and deformed, usually because the body is not getting enough calcium or vitamin D, or both.

scurvy — a disease that causes swollen, bleeding gums, bruised skin, and anemia, because the body is not getting enough vitamin C.

stimulant — a natural or artificial substance that quickly produces a usually temporary increase in energy or activity.

toxin — a poison that is produced by the bodily activities of a living thing and can cause certain kinds of diseases.

More books to read

Eat Smart: A Guide to Good Health for Kids. Dale Figtree (New Win Publishing)

Eat Well. Miriam Moss (Silver Burdett)

Eating Pretty. Elizabeth Karlsberg (Troll Communications)

Energy for Our Bodies. Donna Bailey (Raintree Steck-Vaughn)

Food Power: A Kid's Guide to Eating Right. Alvin Silverstein (Millbrook Press)

Good Morning. Let's Eat. Karin L. Badt (Children's Press)

Nutrition: What's in the Food We Eat? Dorothy H. Patent (Holiday House)

Nutritional Diseases. Bodies in Crisis (series). Jon Zonderman and Laurel Shader (TFC Books)

Staying Healthy: Eating Right. A. B. McGinry (Rosen Group)

Super Snacks. Jean Warren (Warren Publishing)

Vitamins and Minerals. Joan Kalbacken (Children's Press)

Videos

Basic Nutrition: "Let's Make a Meal." (Journal Films & Video)

Can You Tell Me . . . Which Foods Are Good? (Churchill Media)

Choose What You Chew. (New Dimension Media)

Janey Junkfood's Fresh Adventure. (Sunburst Communication)

Look Before You Eat. (Churchill Media)

Nutrition and Diet. Teen Health (series). (Schoolhouse Videos)

Web sites

tqjunior.advanced.org/4485/

www.kidsfood.org/kf_cyber.html

www.fsci.umn.edu/nutrexp/students.htm

www.scurvyboy.com/

Due to the dynamic nature of the Internet, some web sites stay current longer than others. To find additional web sites, use a reliable search engine with one or more of the following keywords: *cholesterol, diets, eating disorders, food, minerals, nutrition, protein, vitamins.*

Index